# Hanukkah

## THIS EDITION

**Produced for DK** by WonderLab Group LLC
Jennifer Emmett, Erica Green, Kate Hale, *Founders*

**Editor** Maya Myers; **Photography Editor** Nicole DiMella; **Managing Editor** Rachel Houghton;
**Designers** Project Design Company; **Researcher** Katie Cederborg; **Copy Editor** Lori Merritt;
**Indexer** Connie Binder; **Proofreader** Susan K. Hom; **Series Reading Specialist** Dr Jennifer Albro;
**Sensitivity Reader** Rabbi Laurie Rice

This edition published in 2025
First published in Great Britain in 2025 by
Dorling Kindersley Limited
20 Vauxhall Bridge Road,
London SW1V 2SA

The authorised representative in the EEA is
Dorling Kindersley Verlag GmbH. Arnulfstr. 124,
80636 Munich, Germany

Copyright © 2025 Dorling Kindersley Limited
10 9 8 7 6 5 4 3 2 1
001–349660–Sep/2025

Published in Great Britain by Dorling Kindersley Limited

A CIP catalogue record for this book
is available from the British Library.
ISBN: 978-0-2417-4125-2

Printed and bound in China

Super Readers Lexile® levels 500L to 610L
Lexile® is the registered trademark of MetaMetrics, Inc. Copyright © 2024 MetaMetrics, Inc. All rights reserved.

The publisher would like to thank the following for their kind permission to reproduce their images:
a=above; c=centre; b=below; l=left; r=right; t=top; b/g=background
**123RF.com:** Malisa Nicolau 3, Tomertu 21; **Adobe Stock:** Simonovstas 11cra; **Alamy Stock Photo:** Eddie Gerald 27, Heritage Image
Partnership Ltd 25cra, History_Docu_Photo 13, ZUMA Press Inc 28b; **Dorling Kindersley:** Barnabas Kindersley 22b; Dreamstime.com:
Ben Hur Photos 22c, Goldenkb 20, Liorpt 1, Elisheva Monasevich 11br, Oksanabratanova 4-5, Tomert 14-15t, 30, Maren Winter 6bl;
**Getty Images:** Anadolu 8, Archive Photos / Hulton Archive 10bl, Hulton Archive / George Pickow 10br, John Lamparski 24, Photodisc /
Nathan Bilow 7, Portland Press Herald 28tl, Universal Images Group / Education Images 29; **Getty Images / iStock:** Chameleonseye
23, DigitalVision Vectors / ZU_09 15br, Dnaveh 16, E+ / Anchiy 25t, E+ / Coldsnowstorm 11clb, E+ / Halbergman 18, FamVeld 17, Scott
Harrison 19cl, Petekarici 9br, Drazen Zigic 19t; **Shutterstock.com:** BrittanyD 26t, Everett Collection 10tl, P Maxwell Photography 12,
Rocharibeiro 26tl, Sergei25 9tl

Cover images: *Front:* **Dreamstime.com:** Tabitazn (Background), Teirin cra;
**Getty Images / iStock:** EyeEm Mobile GmbH; *Back:* **Dreamstime.com:** Teirin cra

## www.dk.com

Level 2

# Hanukkah

Emma Carlson Berne

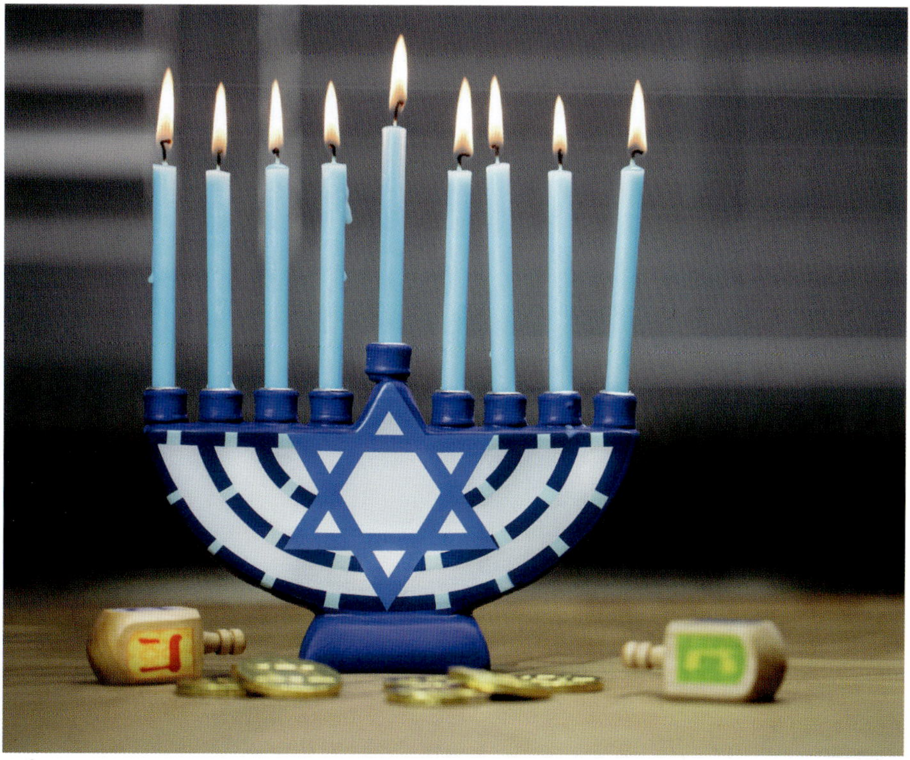

DK

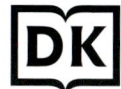

# Contents

# Time to Celebrate

Outside, darkness presses against the windows. But inside, the menorah stands ready to light the winter night. Latkes fry on the cooker. Bags of chocolate gelt lie on the table. Tonight is the first night of Hanukkah.

It's time for candle lighting. The family gathers around the menorah. They light the first candle. They say the blessings.

Then, they place the menorah in a window. It burns brightly there. And the family begins a special Hanukkah meal.

# The Festival of Lights

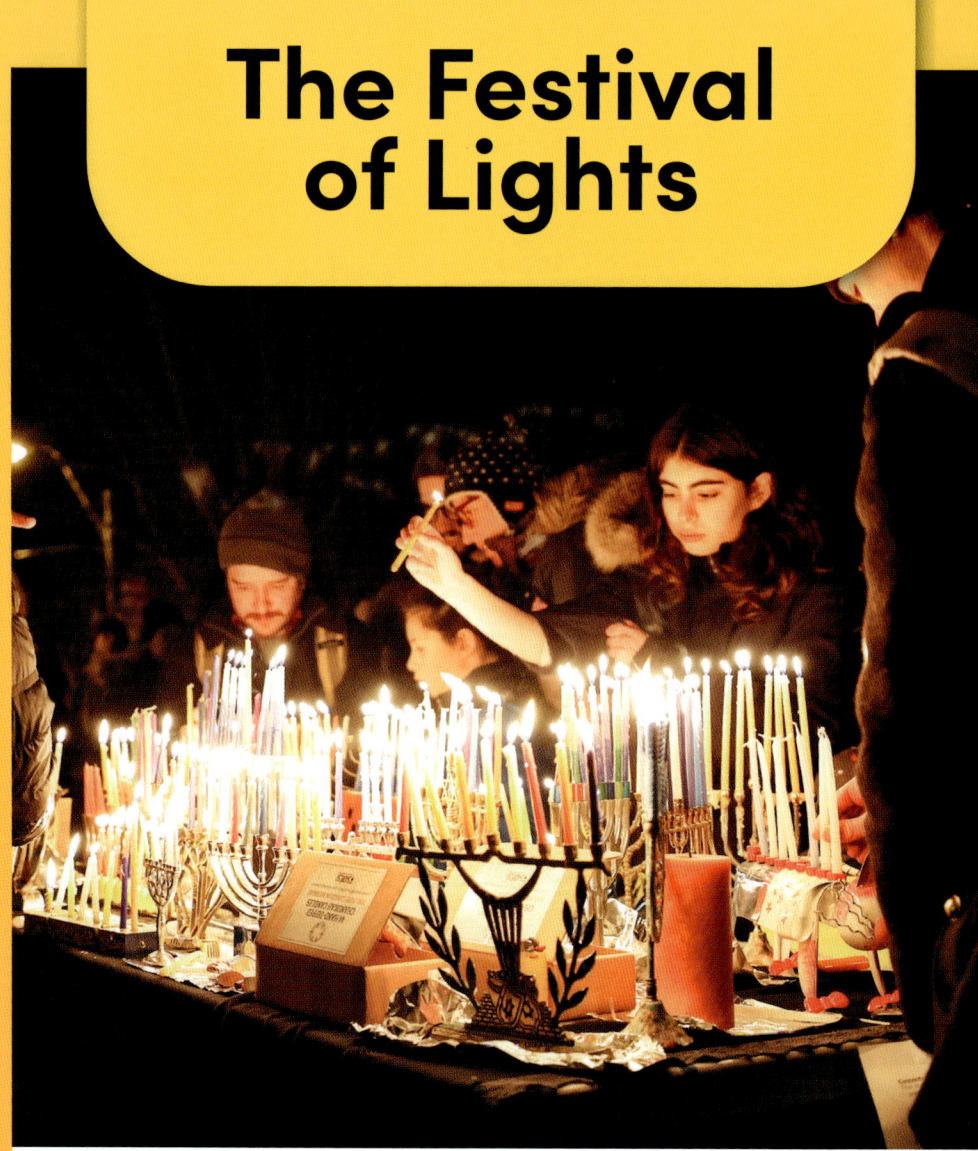

Hanukkah is a holiday. It's observed by Jewish people around the world. It is also called the Festival of Lights.

Hanukkah lasts eight days. It's celebrated according to the Hebrew calendar. The Hebrew calendar is lunisolar. It follows the cycles of the sun and moon. Each month begins with the new moon.

Hanukkah falls in the ninth month of the Hebrew calendar. This is usually in late November to late December on the Western or Gregorian calendar.

HANUKKAH BEGINS AT SUNDOWN

Throughout most of Jewish history, Hanukkah was a minor holiday. Other holidays were more important in the Jewish year.

During the 19th and early 20th centuries, many Jews moved from Europe to the United States. In the US, Christmas was an important holiday. Hanukkah usually falls near Christmas. So, Jewish leaders

encouraged Jewish Americans to celebrate Hanukkah. This was a way of preserving their Jewish heritage in their new country.

## Major Jewish Holidays

Many non-Jewish people think of Hanukkah as the most important Jewish holiday. But these other holidays are very meaningful.

**ROSH HASHANAH** (the Jewish New Year) People celebrate this holiday by eating sweet food. This symbolises a sweet New Year. They also go to synagogue.

**YOM KIPPUR** (the Day of Atonement) Many Jewish people fast during this solemn holiday. They ask forgiveness for things they've done wrong that year.

**PESACH (PASSOVER)** This holiday honours Jewish people's exodus from ancient Egypt. At a special meal called a seder, people eat symbolic food. They read the story of the exodus together.

# Destruction and a Miracle

During Hanukkah, Jewish people remember part of their history. Two thousand years ago in Jerusalem, Greek rulers wanted Jewish people to pray to Greek gods. The Jewish people refused. They wanted to pray to their God.

Judah Maccabee leading the revolt against the Greek army

The Greek army and a Jewish group called the Maccabees fought with each other. The Greek army destroyed the holy temple where the Jews prayed. They broke a sacred oil lamp that was never supposed to go out.

The Maccabees won the fight. But their temple was a mess. They cleaned it and restored it.

The historical story of Hanukkah also contains a legend. The time came to light the sacred lamp. But the lamp needed oil. There was only enough oil to keep the lamp burning for one day.

A messenger ran for more oil. The trip would take him eight days.

Yet the oil lamp kept burning until the messenger returned. The legend says that this was a miracle.

# Celebrating at Home

During Hanukkah, families light candles in a holder called a menorah. The menorah for Hanukkah is called a hanukkiah. It has spaces for eight candles – one for each day of the miracle. There is also a space for a helper candle. In Hebrew, the helper candle is called the shamash. The shamash is lit first. Then, the shamash is used to light the other candles.

One candle is lit for each night of the holiday. On the first night, people light one candle. On the second night, they light two candles. On the last night, they light eight candles. Then, the menorah is glowing. People say special prayers as the candles are lit.

Most people do not blow out Hanukkah candles. The candles are usually allowed to burn down until they go out naturally.

**On Display**

Some people place their lit menorah in a window. This is a way for people to show that they are proud of their Jewish faith.

The menorah is lit. Now, the Hanukkah celebrations begin! Families sing songs while standing around the menorah.

Then, they have a special meal with food that is cooked, or fried, in oil. The oil is a reminder of the oil in the lamp.

Many people fry potato pancakes called latkes. They are often served with apple sauce and sour cream.

Jam doughnuts may be on the table for dessert. The doughnuts are also fried in oil.

Many children play a game called dreidel. The dreidel is a small top. It has Hebrew letters printed on each of the four sides.

To play dreidel, children gather raisins, small sweets, dry beans or coins. They put some of these little things in the middle. This is called the pot.

They take turns spinning the dreidel. The letter that faces up tells the spinner what to do. Nun means they take nothing. Gimel means they take the whole pot. Hay means they take half the pot. Shin means they put one into the pot.

**A Great Miracle**

The letters on the dreidel – nun, gimel, hay and shin – stand for the words in the Hebrew language that mean "a great miracle happened there". This refers to the miracle of the oil in the temple. In Israel, dreidels have the letter peh instead of shin. This means "here" instead of "there".

**NUN (נ)** = take none

**GIMEL (ג)** = take all

**HAY (ה)** = take half

**SHIN/PEH (ש/פ)** = give one

Families often give each other small presents after they light the menorah. Money called gelt is a popular gift. The gelt may be chocolate coins covered in gold foil.

Then, for some families, it's time to sing again.

# Hanukkah Around the World

In some cities, people light huge menorahs in public places. In New York City, a person climbs a ladder to light a giant menorah.

Jewish heroine, Judith

Jewish people in North Africa and some Middle Eastern countries celebrate an extra holiday on the sixth or seventh night of Hanukkah. They remember Jewish women heroines from the past. This celebration is called the Festival of the Daughters.

All over the world, people eat food fried in oil. In Cuba, people make latkes out of plantains instead of potatoes. In some Middle Eastern countries, a fried ball of ground lamb called kibbe is a Hanukkah treat. Some Italian families make fried chicken for their Hanukkah feasts.

In Israel, Hanukkah is a big holiday. Children don't go to school. There are outdoor menorah lightings. People enjoy plays and musical performances. Clear boxes outside homes hold lit menorahs. The glowing candles light up the streets!

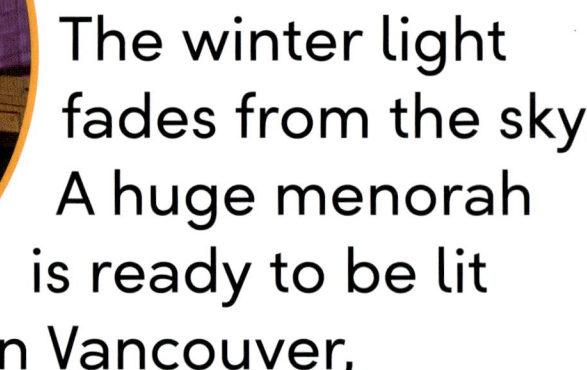

The winter light fades from the sky. A huge menorah is ready to be lit in Vancouver, Washington. A rabbi is raised up on a cherry picker. He lights the menorah!

The community celebrates by building a "canorah". It is made out of cans of food. Later, the food will be donated to a local food bank.

The lights of the giant menorah glow. They are bright in the winter darkness.

Happy Hanukkah!

# Glossary

**Cherry picker**
A type of crane with a platform for raising and lowering people

**Exodus**
The departure of a large group of people from a place; the story of the escape of the ancient Jewish people from Egypt

**Fast**
To not eat or drink during a certain period

**Gregorian calendar**
A solar calendar used in most parts of the world

**Kibbe**
A dish of ground lamb and bulgur formed into balls and fried

**Latkes**
Fried potato and onion pancakes

**Lunisolar**
Relating to both the sun and the moon

**Menorah**
A candleholder with spaces for seven or nine lights. A nine-light menorah used at Hanukkah is also called a hanukkiah.

**Plantain**
A starchy type of banana

**Rabbi**
A Jewish religious leader

**Sacred**
Holy

**Seder**
A religious meal served in Jewish homes to mark the holiday of Passover

**Shamash**
The candle used to light the other candles on a Hanukkah menorah

**Symbolise**
To stand for or represent something

# Index

# Quiz

Answer the questions to see what you have learned. Check your answers in the key below.

1.  How many days does Hanukkah last for?

2.  What was the Jewish rebel group that fought against the Greek army?

3.  True or false: The "helper" candle on the menorah is called the shamash.

4.  You're playing dreidel. It falls on "gimel". What do you get to do with the pot?

5.  What is a common food used to make latkes?

1. . Eight  2. The Maccabees  3. True  4. Take all of it  5. Potatoes